FIRST 50 SONGS
YOU SHOULD PLAY ON THE OBOE

ISBN 978-1-5400-7004-3

Visit Hal Leonard Online at
www.halleonard.com

Contact us:
Hal Leonard
7777 West Bluemound Road
Milwaukee, WI 53213
Email: info@halleonard.com

In Europe, contact:
Hal Leonard Europe Limited
42 Wigmore Street
Marylebone, London, W1U 2RN
Email: info@halleonardeurope.com

In Australia, contact:
Hal Leonard Australia Pty. Ltd.
4 Lentara Court
Cheltenham, Victoria, 3192 Australia
Email: info@halleonard.com.au

ALL OF ME

OBOE

Words and Music by JOHN STEPHENS
and TOBY GAD

Slowly, in 2

ALL YOU NEED IS LOVE

OBOE

Words and Music by JOHN LENNON
and PAUL McCARTNEY

AMAZING GRACE

OBOE

Traditional American Melody

BASIN STREET BLUES

OBOE

Words and Music by
SPENCER WILLIAMS

(small notes optional)

BEST SONG EVER

OBOE

Words and Music by EDWARD DREWETT,
WAYNE HECTOR, JULIAN BUNETTA
and JOHN RYAN

CANON IN D

OBOE

JOHANN PACHELBEL

CARNIVAL OF VENICE

OBOE

By JULIUS BENEDICT

Moderately, with motion

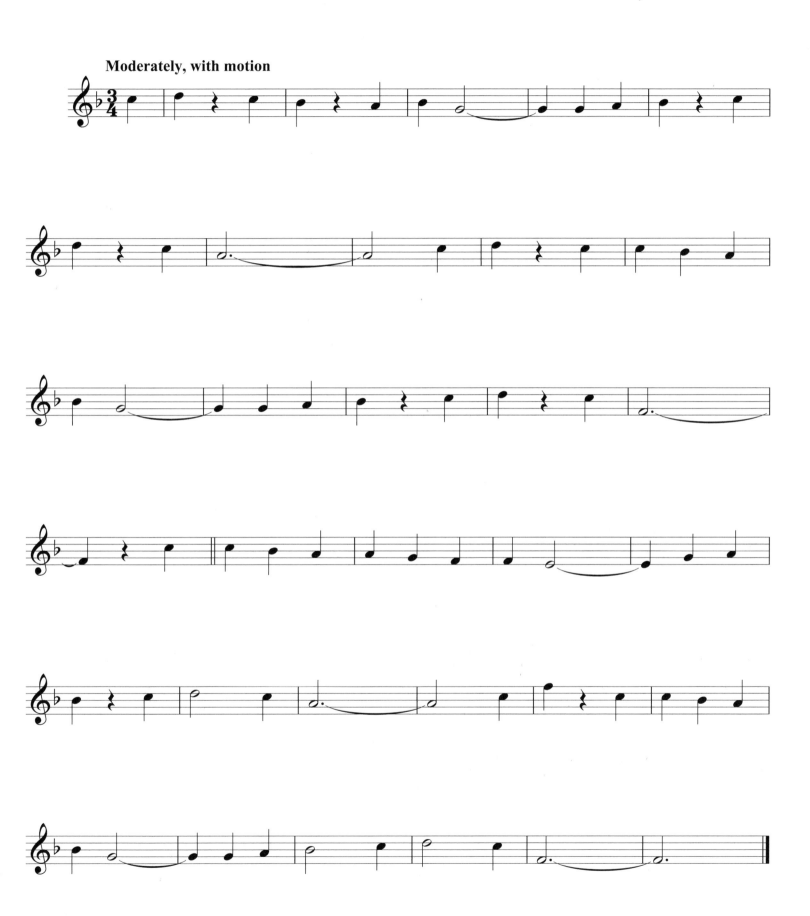

CIRCLE OF LIFE

from THE LION KING

OBOE

Music by ELTON JOHN
Lyrics by TIM RICE

Moderately (with an African beat)

EVERMORE
from BEAUTY AND THE BEAST

OBOE

Music by ALAN MENKEN
Lyrics by TIM RICE

FIGHT SONG

OBOE

Words and Music by RACHEL PLATTEN
and DAVE BASSETT

D.S. al Coda

CODA

FLY ME TO THE MOON
(In Other Words)

OBOE

Words and Music by
BART HOWARD

THE FOOL ON THE HILL

OBOE

Words and Music by JOHN LENNON
and PAUL McCARTNEY

Slowly

FOR ALL WE KNOW

from the Motion Picture LOVERS AND OTHER STRANGERS

OBOE

Words by ROBB WILSON and ARTHUR JAMES
Music by FRED KARLIN

GABRIEL'S OBOE

from the Motion Picture THE MISSION

OBOE

Words and Music by
ENNIO MORRICONE

GOD BLESS AMERICA®

OBOE

Words and Music by
IRVING BERLIN

THE GODFATHER
(Love Theme)
from the Paramount Picture THE GODFATHER

OBOE

By NINO ROTA

Slowly and expressively

HALLELUJAH

OBOE

Words and Music by
LEONARD COHEN

HAPPY
from DESPICABLE ME 2

OBOE

Words and Music by
PHARRELL WILLIAMS

Moderately fast

HAPPY TOGETHER

OBOE

Words and Music by GARRY BONNER
and ALAN GORDON

HELLO

OBOE

Words and Music by
LIONEL RICHIE

Slow Ballad

HELLO, DOLLY!

from HELLO, DOLLY!

OBOE

Music and Lyric by
JERRY HERMAN

HOW DEEP IS YOUR LOVE
from the Motion Picture SATURDAY NIGHT FEVER

OBOE

Words and Music by BARRY GIBB,
ROBIN GIBB and MAURICE GIBB

I WILL ALWAYS LOVE YOU

OBOE

Words and Music by
DOLLY PARTON

Moderately slow

JUST GIVE ME A REASON

Words and Music by ALECIA MOORE,
JEFF BHASKER and NATE RUESS

OBOE

JUST THE WAY YOU ARE

OBOE

Words and Music by BRUNO MARS,
ARI LEVINE, PHILIP LAWRENCE,
KHARI CAIN and KHALIL WALTON

KISS FROM A ROSE

OBOE

Words and Music by
HENRY OLUSEGUN ADEOLA SAMUEL

Flowing

LET IT GO
from FROZEN

OBOE

Music and Lyrics by KRISTEN ANDERSON-LOPEZ
and ROBERT LOPEZ

Slowly, in 2

Fine

D.S. al Fine

MAS QUE NADA

OBOE

Words and Music by
JORGE BEN

MY HEART WILL GO ON
(Love Theme from 'Titanic')
from the Paramount and Twentieth Century Fox Motion Picture TITANIC

OBOE

Music by JAMES HORNER
Lyric by WILL JENNINGS

NATURAL

OBOE

Words and Music by DAN REYNOLDS,
WAYNE SERMON, BEN McKEE,
DANIEL PLATZMAN, JUSTIN TRANTOR,
MATTIAS LARSSON and ROBIN FREDRICKSSON

PURE IMAGINATION
from WILLY WONKA AND THE CHOCOLATE FACTORY

OBOE

Words and Music by LESLIE BRICUSSE
and ANTHONY NEWLEY

NIGHT TRAIN

OBOE

Words by OSCAR WASHINGTON
and LEWIS C. SIMPKINS
Music by JIMMY FORREST

ROAR

OBOE

Words and Music by KATY PERRY,
MAX MARTIN, DR. LUKE,
BONNIE McKEE and HENRY WALTER

ROLLING IN THE DEEP

OBOE

Words and Music by ADELE ADKINS
and PAUL EPWORTH

Moderately

To Coda

D.C. al Coda
(no repeat)

CODA

SATIN DOLL

OBOE

By Duke Ellington

SAY SOMETHING

Words and Music by IAN AXEL,
CHAD VACCARINO and MIKE CAMPBELL

OBOE

Very slowly, in 4

SEE YOU AGAIN

from FURIOUS 7

OBOE

Words and Music by CAMERON THOMAZ,
CHARLIE PUTH, JUSTIN FRANKS,
ANDREW CEDAR, DANN HUME,
JOSH HARDY and PHOEBE COCKBURN

SHAKE IT OFF

OBOE

Words and Music by TAYLOR SWIFT,
MAX MARTIN and SHELLBACK

SHALLOW
from A STAR IS BORN

OBOE

Words and Music by STEFANI GERMANOTTA,
MARK RONSON, ANDREW WYATT
and ANTHONY ROSSOMANDO

Moderately

THE SOUND OF SILENCE

OBOE

Words and Music by
PAUL SIMON

Moderately

STAND BY ME

OBOE

Words and Music by JERRY LEIBER,
MIKE STOLLER and BEN E. KING

Moderately, with a beat

THE STAR-SPANGLED BANNER

OBOE

Words by FRANCIS SCOTT KEY
Music by JOHN STAFFORD SMITH

STAY WITH ME

OBOE

Words and Music by SAM SMITH,
JAMES NAPIER, WILLIAM EDWARD PHILLIPS,
TOM PETTY and JEFF LYNNE

STOMPIN' AT THE SAVOY

OBOE

By BENNY GOODMAN,
EDGAR SAMPSON and CHICK WEBB

SUMMERTIME

from PORGY AND BESS®

OBOE

Music and Lyrics by GEORGE GERSHWIN,
DuBOSE and DOROTHY HEYWARD
and IRA GERSHWIN

SYMPHONY NO. 9 IN E MINOR

("From The New World"), Second Movement Excerpt

OBOE

By ANTONIN DVOŘÁK

WHAT A WONDERFUL WORLD

OBOE

Words and Music by GEORGE DAVID WEISS
and BOB THIELE

TEQUILA

OBOE

By CHUCK RIO

THIS IS ME
from THE GREATEST SHOWMAN

OBOE

Words and Music by BENJ PASEK
and JUSTIN PAUL

UPTOWN FUNK

Words and Music by MARK RONSON,
BRUNO MARS, PHILIP LAWRENCE, JEFF BHASKER, DEVON GALLASPY,
NICHOLAUS WILLIAMS, LONNIE SIMMONS, RONNIE WILSON,
CHARLES WILSON, RUDOLPH TAYLOR and ROBERT WILSON

OBOE